Help with HOMEWORK

motorbike

trumpet

ticket

flowers

bicycle

piano

slide

car

bus

EASY ENGLISH
My World
Vocabulary Book

airport

bird

sun

train

guitar

tree

AUTUMN PUBLISHING

AUTUMN
PUBLISHING

Published in 2020
by Autumn Publishing
Cottage Farm
Sywell
NN6 0BJ
www.autumnpublishing.co.uk

0220 001
2 4 6 8 10 9 7 5 3 1
ISBN 978-1-83852-654-2

Written by Ben Ffrancon Davies
Illustrated by Sue Downing

Designed by Chris Stanley
Edited by Helen Catt

Printed and manufactured in China

EASY ENGLISH

My World

Vocabulary Book

The alphabet

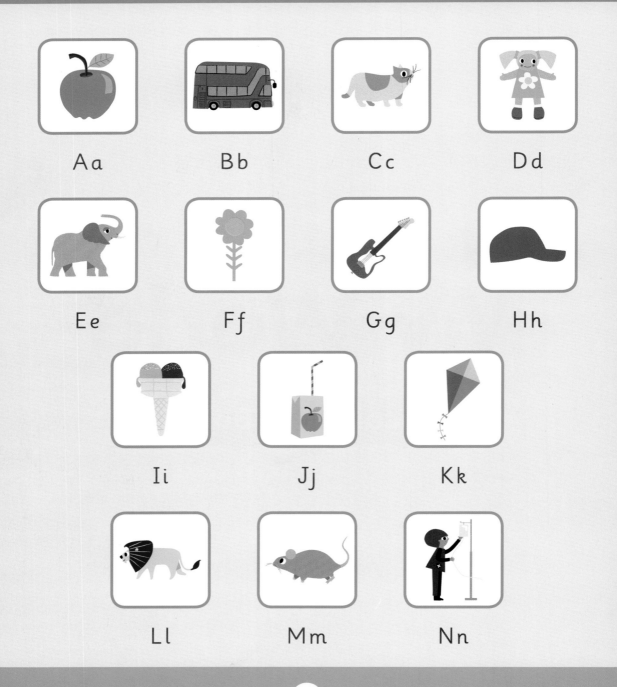

Aa

Bb

Cc

Dd

Ee

Ff

Gg

Hh

Ii

Jj

Kk

Ll

Mm

Nn

Oo

Pp

Qq

Rr

Ss

Tt

Uu

Vv

Ww

Xx

Yy

Zz

Numbers

1 lion

one

2 flamingos

two

3 horses

three

4 tigers

four

5 bears

five

6 dolphins

six

7 penguins

seven

8 dogs

eight

9 cats

nine

Can you count to 20?

10 rabbits

ten

11 lizards

eleven

12 monkeys

twelve

13 snakes

thirteen

14 seagulls

fourteen

15 bats

fifteen

16 mice

sixteen

17 butterflies

seventeen

18 fish

eighteen

19 frogs

nineteen

20 birds

twenty

Colours

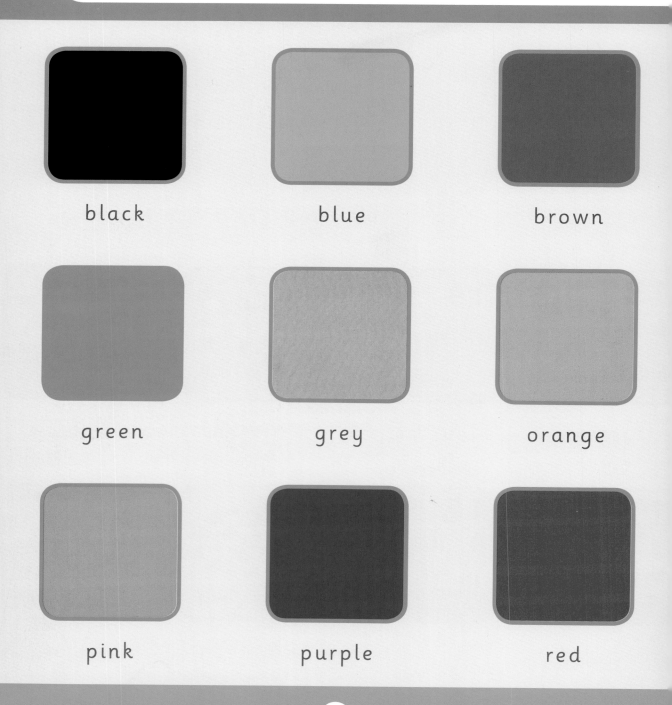

black

blue

brown

green

grey

orange

pink

purple

red

What's your favourite colour?

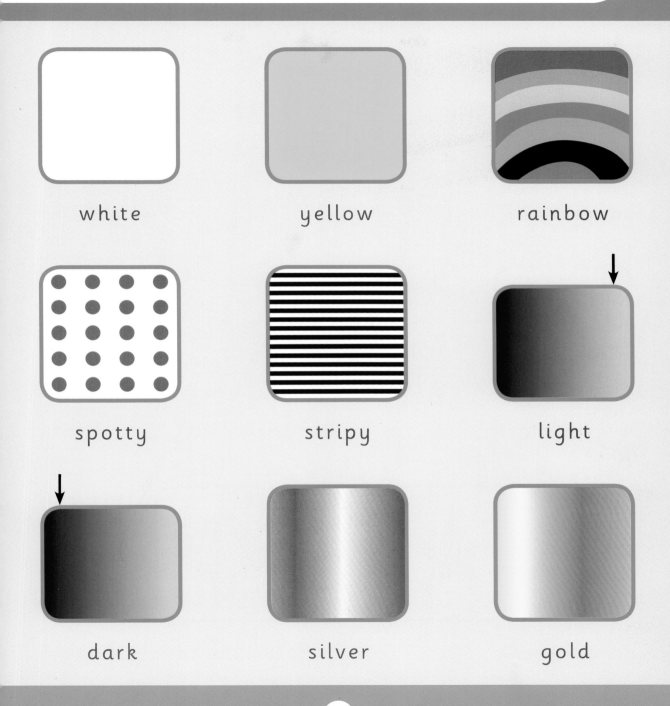

white

yellow

rainbow

spotty

stripy

light

dark

silver

gold

Shapes and sizes

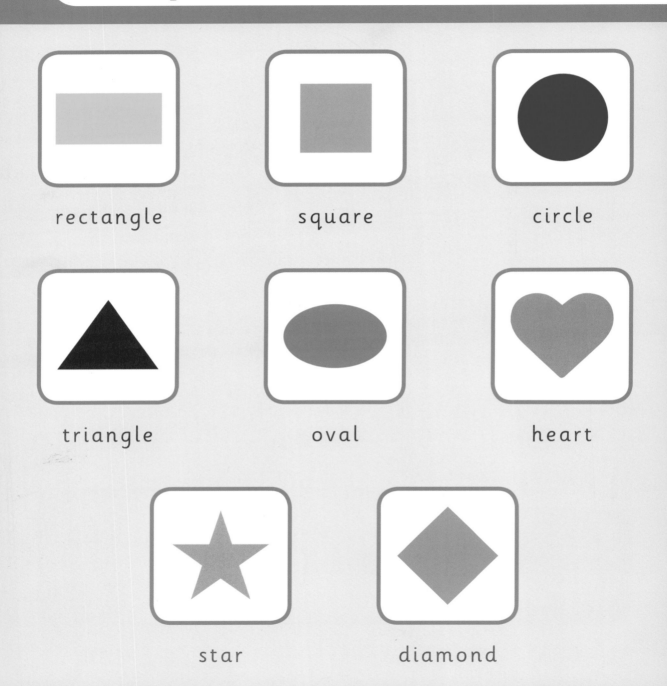

rectangle

square

circle

triangle

oval

heart

star

diamond

Do you know your shapes?

long

short

big

small

At school

school

classroom

computer

desk

book

alphabet

read

write

draw

What's at your school?

teacher

tick

cross

school bag

whiteboard

lesson

chalkboard

student

School subjects

art

English

drama

maths

history

sports

computing

geography

music

What's your favourite subject?

science

playtime

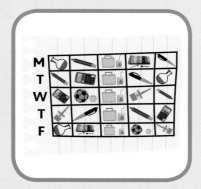

timetable

lunchtime

Jobs

teacher

doctor

nurse

farmer

actor

police
officer

firefighter

chef

dentist

What do you want to be when you grow up?

businesswoman

businessman

builder

pilot

mechanic

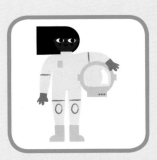

astronaut

plumber

My gadgets

computer

laptop

keyboard

mouse

internet

mobile
phone

tablet

camera

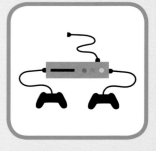

games console

Do you like gadgets?

video game

batteries

plug

headphones

printer

The time

one o'clock

two o'clock

three o'clock

four o'clock

five o'clock

six o'clock

seven o'clock

eight o'clock

nine o'clock

What's the time?

ten o'clock

eleven
o'clock

twelve
o'clock

quarter
past

half past

quarter to

am

pm

Days of the week

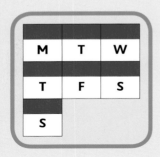

week

Monday

Tuesday

Wednesday

Thursday

Friday

Saturday

Sunday

Weekend

What day is it today?

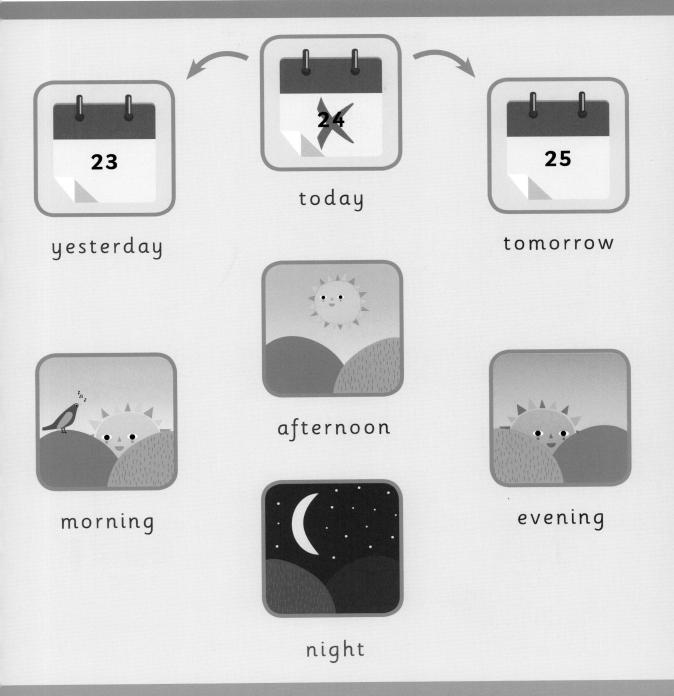

23 | 24 | 25
yesterday | today | tomorrow

morning

afternoon

evening

night

The year

January

February

March

April

May

June

July

August

September

October

November

December

When is your birthday?

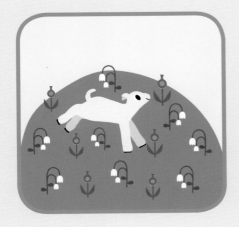

spring

summer

autumn

winter

Around town

shop

playground

park

bookshop

street

zoo

bank

bus stop

café

Where would you like to go?

cinema

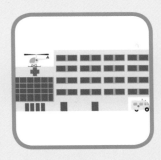

hospital

library

supermarket

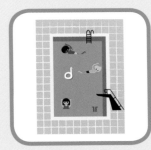

swimming pool

bridge

police station

fire station

railway station

Directions

behind

between

in front of

next to

on

in

under

above

opposite

Which way is the...?

map

left

right

straight on

compass

north

south

east

west

Getting around

car

bike

truck

bus

plane

helicopter

motorbike

ship

train

How do you get around?

drive

fly

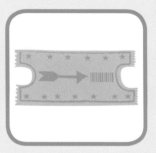

ticket

police car

fire engine

ambulance

airport

bus stop

railway station

At the shops

shopping
bag

trolley

basket

buy

money

credit card

go shopping

shop

market

Shall we go shopping?

till

supermarket

shopping
list

shopping
centre

The weather

sun

cloud

rain

rainbow

snow

wind

fog

storm

What's the weather like today?

It's cloudy.

It's sunny.

It's windy.

It's raining.

It's snowing.

It's stormy.

It's foggy.

At the beach

beach

sea

shell

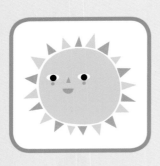
sun

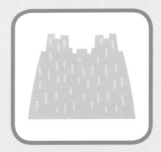
sand castle

sun cream

sunglasses

towel

sand

What's at the beach?

crab

fish

bucket

cave

kite

boat

sailing

surfing

seagull

The countryside

tree

forest

leaves

field

cows

sheep

lake

river

mountain

What's in the countryside?

waterfall

bridge

castle

road

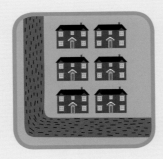

village

grass

flowers

hill

birds

On holiday

beach

countryside

city

passport

plane

mountains

snowman

suitcase

camera

What will you do on holiday?

fishing

shopping

skiing

snowboarding

swimming

taking photos

swimming pool

hotel

Wild animals

crocodile

elephant

giraffe

hippo

lizard

monkey

snake

tiger

bear

What's your favourite animal?

dolphin

kangaroo

koala

lion

panda

parrot

whale

penguin

shark

Sports

badminton

baseball

basketball

cricket

snowboarding

golf

hockey

ice hockey

rugby

Do you do any sports?

skiing

swimming

tennis

table tennis

football

bat

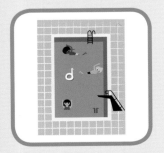
swimming pool

team

ball

Musical instruments

violin

trumpet

guitar

bass

keyboard

harp

flute

drums

piano

Can you play any instruments?

xylophone

clarinet

saxophone

cello

recorder

sing

band

play